UNI

Pontifical Commission
Ecclesia Dei

Instruction

On the application of the Apostolic Letter *Summorum Pontificum* of His Holiness Pope Benedict XVI given *Motu Proprio*

All booklets are published thanks to the generous support of the members of the Catholic Truth Society

CATHOLIC TRUTH SOCIETY
PUBLISHERS TO THE HOLY SEE

Contents

Universae Ecclesiae - Latin 3

Universae Ecclesiae - English 17

Motu Proprio *Summorum Pontificum* - Latin 31

Motu Proprio *Summorum Pontificum* - English 39

Accompanying Letter of His Holiness Benedict XVI
to the Bishops 48

UNIVERSAE ECCLESIAE

Pontificia Commissio
Ecclesia Dei

INSTRUCTIO

Ad exsequendas Litteras Apostolicas *Summorum Pontificum* a S. S. BENEDICTO PP. XVI Motu Proprio datas

I.
Prooemium

1. Universæ Ecclesiæ Litteræ Apostolicæ *Summorum Pontificum* Benedicti PP. XVI, die 7 iulii a. D. 2007 motu proprio datæ atque inde a die 14 septembris a. D. 2007 vigentes, Romanæ Liturgiæ divitias reddiderunt propiores.

2. Hisce Litteris Motu Proprio datis Summus Pontifex Benedictus XVI legem universalem Ecclesiæ tulit ut regulis nostris temporibus aptioribus quoad usum Romanæ Liturgiæ anno 1962 vigentem provideret.

3. Sedula Summorum Pontificum sollicitudine hac in Sacræ Liturgiæ cura necnon et in recognoscendis liturgicis libris memorata, Sanctitas Sua antiquum principium in mentem revocavit, ab immemorabilibus receptum et in futurum servandum: "*unaquæque Ecclesia particularis concordare debet cum universali Ecclesia non solum*

quoad fidei doctrinam et signa sacramentalia, sed etiam quoad usus universaliter acceptos ab apostolica et continua traditione, qui servandi sunt non solum ut errores vitentur, verum etiam ad fidei integritatem tradendam, quia Ecclesiæ lex orandi eius legi credendi respondet"[1].

4. Insuper, Apostolicus Dominus et Romanos Pontifices commemorat, qui hac in cura maximopere meriti sunt, præsertim S. Gregorium Magnum et S. Pium V. Summus Pontifex etiam recolit inter liturgicos libros, *Missale Romanum* semper eminuisse, prolabentibusque sæculis incrementa novisse, usque ad beatum Papam Ioannem XXIII. Deinde, cum instauratio liturgica post Concilium Vaticanum II ageretur, Paulus VI anno 1970 novum Missale usui Ecclesiæ Ritus Latini destinatum adprobavit, quod postea in plures linguas translatum fuit cuiusque editio tertia anno 2000 a Ioanne Paulo II est promulgata.

5. Nonnulli vero Christifideles, spiritu rituum liturgicorum Concilio Vaticano II anteriorum imbuti, desiderium præcipuum patefecerant antiquam servandi traditionem. Quam ob rem Ioannes Paulus II, speciali Indulto a Sacra Congregatione pro Sacramentis et Cultu Divino anno 1984 concesso, "*Quattuor abhinc annos*", facultatem dedit utendi Missali Romano a beato Papa Ioanne XXIII promulgato, attentis tamen quibusdam

---

[1] BENEDICTUS XVI, *Litterae Apostolicae Summorum Pontificum Motu Proprio datae*, I, AAS 99 (2007) 777; cf. *Institutio Generalis Missalis Romani*, tertia editio 2002, n. 397.

conditionibus. Præterea ipse Ioannes Paulus II Litteris Apostolicis *Ecclesia Dei* motu proprio anno 1988 datis, Episcopos ad magnanimem liberalitatem huius facultatis concedendæ, ad bonum omnium christifidelium id postulantium, adhortatus est. Similiter et Papa Benedictus XVI promulgando Litteras Apostolicas *Summorum Pontificum* nuncupatas egit, de quibus vero quædam principia essentialia ad Usum spectantia Antiquiorem Ritus Romani quam maxime heic recolere præstat.

6. Textus Missalis Romani a Paulo VI promulgati, et textus ad ultimam usque editionem Ioannis XXIII pertinentes, duæ expressiones Liturgiæ Romanæ exstant, quæ respective *ordinaria* et *extraordinaria* nuncupantur: agitur nempe de duobus unius Ritus Romani usibus, qui ad invicem iuxta ponuntur. Nam utraque forma est expressio unicæ Ecclesiæ legis orandi. Propter venerabilem et antiquum usum *forma extraordinaria* debito honore est servanda.

7. Litteras Apostolicas *Summorum Pontificum* motu proprio datas comitatur Epistola ab ipso Summo Pontifice eodem die subsignata (7. VII. 2007), in qua fuse de opportunitate necnon et de necessitate ipsarum Litterarum agitur: leges recentiores erant nempe ferendæ, deficientibus regulis quæ usum Liturgiæ Romanæ anno 1962 vigentem plane ordinarent. Insuper recentiore legislatione opus erat quia, edito novo Missali, non est visum cur regulæ edendæ essent

quoad usum Liturgiæ anni 1962. Increscentibus magis magisque in dies fidelibus expostulantibus celebrationem *formæ extraordinariæ*, leges autem erant ferendæ. Inter cetera monet Benedictus XVI: "*Inter duas Missalis Romani editiones nulla est contradictio. In historia liturgiæ incrementum et progressus inveniuntur, nulla tamen ruptura. Id quod maioribus nostris sacrum erat, nobis manet sacrum et grande, et non licet ut repente omnino vetitum sit, neque ut plane noxium judicetur*"[2].

8. Litteræ Apostolicæ *Summorum Pontificum* eminenter exprimunt Magisterium Romani Pontificis eiusque munus regendi atque Sacram Liturgiam ordinandi[3], ipsiusque sollicitudinem utpote Christi Vicarii et Ecclesiæ Universæ Pastoris[4]. Ipsæ Litteræ intendunt:

a) Liturgiam Romanam in Antiquiori Usu, prout pretiosum thesaurum servandum, omnibus largire fidelibus;

b) Usum eiusdem Liturgiæ iis re vera certum facere, qui id petunt, considerando ipsum Usum Liturgiæ Romanæ anno 1962 vigentem esse facultatem ad bonum fidelium datam, ac proinde in favorem fidelium benigne esse interpretandam, quibus præcipue destinatur;

c) Reconciliationi in sinu Ecclesiæ favere.

---

2. BENEDICTUS XVI, *Epistola ad Episcopos ad producendas Litteras Apostolicas Motu Proprio datas, de Usu Liturgiae Romanae Instaurationi anni 1970 praecedentis*, AAS 99 (2007) 798.

3. Cf. CIC, can. 838 § 1 et § 2.

4. Cf. CIC, can. 331.

II.

Munera Pontificiæ Commissionis *Ecclesia Dei*

9. Summus Pontifex Pontificiæ Commissioni *Ecclesia Dei* potestatem ordinariam vicariam dignatus est impertire in omnibus rebus intra eius competentiæ fines, præsertim circa sedulam observantiam et vigilantiam in exsequendas dispositiones in Litteris Apostolicis *Summorum Pontificum* contentas (cf. art. 12).

10. § 1. Præter facultates olim a Ioanne Paulo II concessas necnon a Benedicto XVI confirmatas (cf. Litteræ Apostolicæ *Summorum Pontificum*, art.11 et art.12), Pontificia Commissio huiusmodi potestatem exercet etiam in decernendo de recursibus ei legitime commissis, prout hierarchicus Superior, adversus actum administrativum singularem a quolibet Ordinario emissum, qui Litteris Apostolicis videatur contrarius.

§ 2. Decreta quæ Pontificia Commissio de recursibus emanat, apud Supremum Tribunal Signaturæ Apostolicæ oppugnari possunt ad normam iuris.

11. Pontificiæ Commissionis *Ecclesia Dei*, prævia adprobatione Congregationis pro Cultu Divino et Disciplina Sacramentorum, est curare de edendis libris liturgicis ad *formam extraordinariam* Ritus Romani pertinentibus.

III.

Normæ Præcipuæ

12. Pontifícia hæc Commissio, vigore auctoritatis sibi commissæ et facultatum quibus gaudet, peracta inquisitione apud Episcopos totius orbis, rectam interpretationem et fidelem exsecutionem Litterarum Apostolicarum *Summorum Pontificum* pro certo habere volens, hanc Instructionem edit, ad normam canonis 34 Codicis Iuris Canonici.

De Episcoporum Dioecesanorum Competentia

13. Episcoporum Dioecesanorum, iuxta Codicem Iuris Canonici, est vigilare circa rem liturgicam, ut bonum commune servetur et ut omnia digne, pacifice et æquo animo in eorum Dioecesibus fiant[5], iuxta mentem Romani Pontificis in Litteris Apostolicis *Summorum Pontificum* palam expressam[6]. Si quæ controversia oriatur vel dubium fundatum quoad celebrationem *formæ extraordinariæ*, iudicium Pontificiæ Commissioni *Ecclesia Dei* reservatur.

14. Episcopo Dioecesano munus incumbit necessaria suppeditandi subsidia ut fidelis erga formam extraordinariam Ritus Romani habeatur observantia, ad normam Litterarum Apostolicarum *Summorum Pontificum*.

---

[5] Cf. CIC, cann. 223, § 2; 838 § 1 et § 4.

[6] Cf. BENEDICTUS XVI, *Epistola ad Episcopos ad producendas Litteras Apostolicas Motu Proprio datas, de Usu Liturgiae Romanae Instaurationi anni 1970 praecedentis*, AAS 99 (2007) 799.

De coetu fidelium (cf. Litteræ Apostolicæ *Summorum Pontificum*, art. 5 § 1)

15. Coetus fidelium dicitur "stabiliter exsistens" ad sensum art. 5 § 1 Litterarum Apostolicarum *Summorum Pontificum*, quando ab aliquibus personis cuiusdam paroeciæ constituitur, etsi post publicationem Litterarum Apostolicarum coniunctis, ratione venerationis Liturgiæ in Antiquiore Usu, poscentibus ut in ecclesia paroeciali vel in aliquo oratorio vel sacello Antiquior Usus celebretur: hic coetus constitui potest a personis ex pluribus paroeciis aut dioecesibus convenientibus et qui una concurrunt ad ecclesiam paroecialem aut oratorium ad finem, de quo supra, assequendum.

16. Si quidam sacerdos obiter in quandam ecclesiam paroecialem vel oratorium cum aliquibus personis incidens, Sacrum in *forma extraordinaria* facere velit, ad normam artt. 2 et 4 Litterarum Apostolicarum, parochus aut rector ecclesiæ, vel sacerdos qui de ea curam gerit, ad celebrandum admittat, attento tamen ordine celebrationum liturgicarum ipsius ecclesiæ.

17. § 1. Ut de singulis casibus iudicium feratur, parochus aut rector, aut sacerdos qui ecclesiæ curam habet, prudenti mente agat, pastorali zelo, caritate et urbanitate suffultus.

§ 2. Si coetus paucis constet fidelibus, ad Ordinarium loci adeundum est ut designet ecclesiam in quam ad huiusmodi celebrationes fideles se conferre possint, ita ut actuosa participatio facilior et Sanctæ Missæ celebratio dignior reddi valeant.

18. In sanctuariis et in peregrinationum locis possibilitas celebrandi secundum *extraordinariam formam* coetibus peregrinorum id petentibus præbeatur (cf. Litteræ Apostolicæ *Summorum Pontificum*, art. 5 § 3), si sacerdos adest idoneus.

19. Christifideles celebrationem secundum *formam extraordinariam* postulantes, auxilium ne ferant neque nomen dent consociationibus, quæ validitatem vel legitimitatem Sanctæ Missæ Sacrificii et Sacramentorum secundum *formam ordinariam* impugnent, vel Romano Pontifici, Universæ Ecclesiæ Pastori quoquo modo sint infensæ.

De Sacerdotibus idoneis (cf. Litteræ Apostolicæ *Summorum Pontificum*, art. 5 § 4)

20. Quoad ea quæ necessaria sunt ut sacerdos quidam idoneus habeatur ad celebrandum secundum *formam extraordinariam*, statuitur:

a) Quivis sacerdos, ad normam Iuris Canonici[7], non impeditus, idoneus censetur ad celebrandam Sanctam Missam secundum *formam extraordinariam*;

---

[7] Cf. CIC, can. 900, § 2.

b) ad usum Latini sermonis quod attinet, necesse est ut sacerdos celebraturus scientia polleat ad verba recte proferenda eorumque intelligendam significationem;

c) quoad peritiam vero ritus exsequendi, idonei habentur sacerdotes qui ad Sacrum faciendum secundum *extraordinariam formam* sponte adeunt et qui antea hoc fecerant.

21. Ordinarii enixe rogantur ut clericis instituendis occasionem præbeant accommodatam artem celebrandi in *forma extraordinaria* acquirendi, quod potissimum pro Seminariis valet, in quibus providebitur ut sacrorum alumni convenienter instituantur, Latinum discendo sermonem[8] et, adiunctis id postulantibus, ipsam Ritus Romani *formam extraordinariam*.

22. In Dioecesibus ubi desint sacerdotes idonei, fas est Episcopis dioecesanis iuvamen a sacerdotibus Institutorum a Pontificia Commissione *Ecclesia Dei* erectorum exposcere, sive ut celebrent, sive ut ipsam artem celebrandi doceant.

23. Facultas celebrandi Missam sine populo seu uno tantum ministro participante, secundum *formam extraordinariam* Ritus Romani concessa est cuivis presbytero, tum sæculari, cum religioso (cf. Litteræ Apostolicæ *Summorum Pontificum*, art. 2). Ergo, in

---

8. Cf. CIC, can. 249; cf. Conc. Vat. II, Const. *Sacrosanctum Concilium*, n. 36; Decl. *Optatam totius* n. 13.

huiusmodi celebrationibus, sacerdotes, ad normam Litterarum Apostolicarum, nulla speciali licentia Ordinariorum vel superiorum indigent.

De disciplina liturgica et ecclesiastica

24. Libri liturgici *formæ extraordinariæ* adhibeantur ut prostant. Omnes qui secundum *extraordinariam formam* Ritus Romani celebrare exoptant, tenentur rubricas relativas scire easque in celebrationibus recte exsequi.

25. In antiquo Missali recentiores sancti et aliquæ ex novis præfationibus inseri possunt immo debent[9], secundum quod quam primum statutum erit.

26. Ad ea quæ constabilita sunt in Litteris Apostolicis *Summorum Pontificum*, ad articulum 6, dicendum est quod lectiones Sanctæ Missæ, quæ in Missali anni 1962 continentur, proferri possunt aut solum Latine, aut Latine, vernacula sequente versione, aut in Missis lectis etiam solum vernacule.

27. Quoad regulas disciplinares ad celebrationem *formæ extraordinariæ* pertinentes, applicetur disciplina ecclesiastica Codicis Iuris Canonici anno 1983 promulgati.

28. Præterea, cum sane de lege speciali agitur, quoad materiam propriam, Litteræ Apostolicæ *Summorum Pontificum* derogant omnibus legibus liturgicis, sacrorum

---

[9] Cf. BENEDICTUS XVI, *Epistola ad Episcopos ad producendas Litteras Apostolicas Motu Proprio datas, de Usu Liturgiae Romanae Instaurationi anni 1970 praecedentis*, AAS 99 (2007) 797.

rituum propriis, exinde ab anno 1962 promulgatis, et cum rubricis librorum liturgicorum anni 1962 non congruentibus.

De Confirmatione et de Ordine

29. Facultas adhibendi formulam antiquam ad Confirmationem impertiendam, confirmata est a Litteris Apostolicis *Summorum Pontificum* (cf. art. 9, § 2), proinde non necessario adhibenda est pro forma *extraordinaria* formula recentior, quæ in *Ordine Confirmationis* Pauli PP. VI invenitur.

30. Quoad primam Tonsuram, Ordines Minores et Subdiaconatum, Litteræ Apostolicæ *Summorum Pontificum* nullam obmutationem in disciplina Codicis Iuris Canonici anno 1983 introduxerunt: hac de causa, pro Institutis Vitæ Consecratæ et Societatibus Vitæ Apostolicæ Pontificiæ Commissioni *Ecclesia Dei* subditis, sodalis votis perpetuis professus aut societati clericali vitæ apostolicæ definitive incorporatus, per receptum diaconatum incardinatur tamquam clericus eidem instituto aut societati, ad normam canonis 266 § 2 Codicis Iuris Canonici.

31. Dumtaxat Institutis Vitæ Consecratæ et Societatibus Vitæ Apostolicæ Pontificiæ Commissioni *Ecclesia Dei* subditis, et his ubi servatur usus librorum liturgicorum *formæ extraordinariæ*, licet Pontificali Romano anni 1962 uti ad Ordines maiores et minores conferendos.

De Breviario Romano

32. Omnibus clericis conceditur facultas recitandi Breviarium Romanum anni 1962, de quo art. 9, § 3 Litterarum Apostolicarum *Summorum Pontificum*, et quidem integre et Latino sermone.

De Triduo Sacro

33. Coetus fidelium, anteriori traditioni liturgicæ adhærens, iure gaudet, si sacerdos idoneus adest, celebrandi et ipsum Sacrum Triduum iuxta *extraordinariam formam*. Deficiente autem ecclesia vel oratorio ad huiusmodi celebrationes exsequendas exclusive deputatis, parochus aut Ordinarius, communi de consilio cum idoneo sacerdote, favorabiliores præbeant occasiones pro bono animarum assequendo, haud exclusa possibilitate reiterandi Sacri Tridui celebrationes in ipsa ecclesia.

De Ritibus Religiosorum Ordinum

34. Sodalibus Ordinum Religiosorum licet uti propriis libris liturgicis anno 1962 vigentibus.

De Pontificali Romano et de Rituali Romano

35. Salvo quod sub n. 31 huius Instructionis præscriptum est, ad mentem n. 28 ipsius Instructionis licet Pontificale Romanum, Rituale Romanum et Cæremoniale Episcoporum anno 1962 vigentia adhibere.

Summus Pontifex Benedictus PP. XVI, in Audientia die 8 aprilis a. d. MMXI subscripto Cardinali Præsidi Pontificiæ Commissionis "Ecclesia Dei" *concessa, hanc Instructionem ratam habuit et publici iuris fieri iussit.*

Datum Romæ, ex Aedibus Pontificiæ Commissionis *Ecclesia Dei*, die 30 aprilis a. D. MMXI, in memoria S. Pii V.

Gulielmus Cardinalis Levada
Præses

Vido Pozzo
A Secretis

UNIVERSAE ECCLESIAE

Pontifical Commission *Ecclesia Dei*

INSTRUCTION

On the application of the Apostolic Letter *Summorum Pontificum* of HIS HOLINESS POPE BENEDICT XVI given *Motu Proprio*

I.

Introduction

1. The Apostolic Letter *Summorum Pontificum* of the Sovereign Pontiff Benedict XVI given *Motu Proprio* on 7 July 2007, which came into effect on 14 September 2007, has made the richness of the Roman Liturgy more accessible to the Universal Church.

2. With this Motu Proprio, the Holy Father Pope Benedict XVI promulgated a universal law for the Church, intended to establish new regulations for the use of the Roman Liturgy in effect in 1962.

3. The Holy Father, having recalled the concern of the Sovereign Pontiffs in caring for the Sacred Liturgy and in their recognition of liturgical books, reaffirms the

traditional principle, recognised from time immemorial and necessary to be maintained into the future, that "*each particular Church must be in accord with the universal Church not only regarding the doctrine of the faith and sacramental signs, but also as to the usages universally handed down by apostolic and unbroken tradition. These are to be maintained not only so that errors may be avoided, but also so that the faith may be passed on in its integrity, since the Church's rule of prayer* (lex orandi) *corresponds to her rule of belief* (lex credendi)."[1]

4. The Holy Father recalls also those Roman Pontiffs who, in a particular way, were notable in this task, specifically Saint Gregory the Great and Saint Pius V. The Holy Father stresses moreover that, among the sacred liturgical books, the *Missale Romanum* has enjoyed a particular prominence in history, and was kept up to date throughout the centuries until the time of Blessed Pope John XXIII. Subsequently in 1970, following the liturgical reform after the Second Vatican Council, Pope Paul VI approved for the Church of the Latin rite a new Missal, which was then translated into various languages. In the year 2000, Pope John Paul II promulgated the third edition of this Missal.

---

1. BENEDICTUS XVI, *Litterae Apostolicae Summorum Pontificum motu proprio datae*, I, AAS 99 (2007) 777; cf. *Institutio Generalis Missalis Romani*, tertia editio 2002, n. 397.

5. Many of the faithful, formed in the spirit of the liturgical forms prior to the Second Vatican Council, expressed a lively desire to maintain the ancient tradition. For this reason, Pope John Paul II with a special Indult *Quattuor abhinc annos* issued in 1984 by the Congregation for Divine Worship, granted the faculty under certain conditions to restore the use of the Missal promulgated by Blessed Pope John XXIII. Subsequently, Pope John Paul II, with the Motu Proprio *Ecclesia Dei* of 1988, exhorted the Bishops to be generous in granting such a faculty for all the faithful who requested it. Pope Benedict continues this policy with the Motu Proprio *Summorum Pontificum* regarding certain essential criteria for the *Usus Antiquior* of the Roman Rite, which are recalled here.

6. The Roman Missal promulgated by Pope Paul VI and the last edition prepared under Pope John XXIII, are two forms of the Roman Liturgy, defined respectively as *ordinaria* and *extraordinaria*: they are two usages of the one Roman Rite, one alongside the other. Both are the expression of the same *lex orandi* of the Church. On account of its venerable and ancient use, the *forma extraordinaria* is to be maintained with appropriate honour.

7. The Motu Proprio *Summorum Pontificum* was accompanied by a letter from the Holy Father to Bishops, with the same date as the Motu Proprio (7 July 2007).

This letter gave further explanations regarding the appropriateness and the need for the Motu Proprio; it was a matter of overcoming a lacuna by providing new norms for the use of the Roman Liturgy of 1962. Such norms were needed particularly on account of the fact that, when the new Missal had been introduced under Pope Paul VI, it had not seemed necessary to issue guidelines regulating the use of the 1962 Liturgy. By reason of the increase in the number of those asking to be able to use the *forma extraordinaria*, it has become necessary to provide certain norms in this area.

Among the statements of the Holy Father was the following: "*There is no contradiction between the two editions of the Roman Missal. In the history of the Liturgy growth and progress are found, but not a rupture. What was sacred for prior generations, remains sacred and great for us as well, and cannot be suddenly prohibited altogether or even judged harmful.*"[2]

8. The Motu Proprio *Summorum Pontificum* constitutes an important expression of the Magisterium of the Roman Pontiff and of his *munus* of regulating and ordering the Church's Sacred Liturgy.[3] The Motu Proprio manifests his solicitude as Vicar of Christ and Supreme Pastor of the Universal Church,[4] and has the aim of:

---

2. BENEDICTUS XVI, *Epistola ad Episcopos ad producendas Litteras Apostolicas motu proprio datas, de Usu Liturgiae Romanae Instaurationi anni 1970 praecedentis*, AAS 99 (2007) 798.

3. Cf. *Code of Canon Law*, Canon 838 §1 and §2.

4. Cf. *Code of Canon Law*, Canon 331.

a.) offering to all the faithful the Roman Liturgy in the *Usus Antiquior*, considered as a precious treasure to be preserved;

b.) effectively guaranteeing and ensuring the use of the *forma extraordinaria* for all who ask for it, given that the use of the 1962 Roman Liturgy is a faculty generously granted for the good of the faithful and therefore is to be interpreted in a sense favourable to the faithful who are its principal addressees;

c.) promoting reconciliation at the heart of the Church.

II.
The Responsibilities of the Pontifical Commission Ecclesia Dei

9. The Sovereign Pontiff has conferred upon the Pontifical Commission *Ecclesia Dei* ordinary vicarious power for the matters within its competence, in a particular way for monitoring the observance and application of the provisions of the Motu Proprio *Summorum Pontificum* (cf. art. 12).

10. § 1. The Pontifical Commission exercises this power, beyond the faculties previously granted by Pope John Paul II and confirmed by Pope Benedict XVI (cf. Motu Proprio *Summorum Pontificum*, artt. 11-12), also by means of the power to decide upon recourses legitimately sent to it, as hierarchical Superior, against any possible

singular administrative provision of an Ordinary which appears to be contrary to the Motu Proprio.

§ 2. The decrees by which the Pontifical Commission decides recourses may be challenged *ad normam iuris* before the Supreme Tribunal of the Apostolic Signatura.

11. After having received the approval from the Congregation for Divine Worship and the Discipline of the Sacraments, the Pontifical Commission *Ecclesia Dei* will have the task of looking after future editions of liturgical texts pertaining to the *forma extraordinaria* of the Roman Rite.

III.
Specific Norms

12. Following upon the inquiry made among the Bishops of the world, and with the desire to guarantee the proper interpretation and the correct application of the Motu Proprio *Summorum Pontificum*, this Pontifical Commission, by virtue of the authority granted to it and the faculties which it enjoys, issues this Instruction according to can. 34 of the *Code of Canon Law*.

The Competence of Diocesan Bishops

13. Diocesan Bishops, according to Canon Law, are to monitor liturgical matters in order to guarantee the common good and to ensure that everything is proceeding

in peace and serenity in their Dioceses[5], always in agreement with the *mens* of the Holy Father clearly expressed by the Motu Proprio *Summorum Pontificum*.[6] In cases of controversy or well-founded doubt about the celebration in the *forma extraordinaria*, the Pontifical Commission *Ecclesia Dei* will adjudicate.

14. It is the task of the Diocesan Bishop to undertake all necessary measures to ensure respect for the *forma extraordinaria* of the Roman Rite, according to the Motu Proprio *Summorum Pontificum*.

The *coetus fidelium* (cf. Motu Proprio *Summorum Pontificum*, art. 5 § 1)

15. A *coetus fidelium* ("group of the faithful") can be said to be *stabiliter existens* ("existing in a stable manner"), according to the sense of art. 5 § 1 of the Motu Proprio *Summorum Pontificum*, when it is constituted by some people of an individual parish who, even after the publication of the Motu Proprio, come together by reason of their veneration for the Liturgy in the *Usus Antiquior*, and who ask that it might be celebrated in the parish church or in an oratory or chapel; such a *coetus* ("group") can also be composed of persons coming from different

---

5. Cf. *Code of Canon Law*, Canons 223 § 2 or 838 §1 and §4.

6. BENEDICTUS XVI, *Epistola ad Episcopos ad producendas Litteras Apostolicas motu proprio datas, de Usu Liturgiae Romanae Instaurationi anni 1970 praecedentis*, AAS 99 (2007) 799.

parishes or dioceses, who gather together in a specific parish church or in an oratory or chapel for this purpose.

16. In the case of a priest who presents himself occasionally in a parish church or an oratory with some faithful, and wishes to celebrate in the *forma extraordinaria*, as foreseen by articles 2 and 4 of the Motu Proprio *Summorum Pontificum*, the pastor or rector of the church, or the priest responsible, is to permit such a celebration, while respecting the schedule of liturgical celebrations in that same church.

17. § 1. In deciding individual cases, the pastor or the rector, or the priest responsible for a church, is to be guided by his own prudence, motivated by pastoral zeal and a spirit of generous welcome.

§ 2. In cases of groups which are quite small, they may approach the Ordinary of the place to identify a church in which these faithful may be able to come together for such celebrations, in order to ensure easier participation and a more worthy celebration of the Holy Mass.

18. Even in sanctuaries and places of pilgrimage the possibility to celebrate in the *forma extraordinaria* is to be offered to groups of pilgrims who request it (cf. Motu Proprio *Summorum Pontificum*, art. 5 § 3), if there is a qualified priest.

19. The faithful who ask for the celebration of the *forma extraordinaria* must not in any way support or belong to groups which show themselves to be against the validity

or legitimacy of the Holy Mass or the Sacraments celebrated in the *forma ordinaria* or against the Roman Pontiff as Supreme Pastor of the Universal Church.

Sacerdos idoneus ("Qualified Priest") (cf. Motu Proprio *Summorum Pontificum*, art 5 § 4)

20. With respect to the question of the necessary requirements for a priest to be held *idoneus* ("qualified") to celebrate in the *forma extraordinaria*, the following is hereby stated:

a.) Every Catholic priest who is not impeded by Canon Law[7] is to be considered *idoneus* ("qualified") for the celebration of the Holy Mass in the *forma extraordinaria*.

b.) Regarding the use of the Latin language, a basic knowledge is necessary, allowing the priest to pronounce the words correctly and understand their meaning.

c.) Regarding knowledge of the execution of the Rite, priests are presumed to be qualified who present themselves spontaneously to celebrate the *forma extraordinaria*, and have celebrated it previously.

21. Ordinaries are asked to offer their clergy the possibility of acquiring adequate preparation for celebrations in the *forma extraordinaria*. This applies also to Seminaries, where future priests should be given proper formation, including study of Latin[8] and, where

7. Cf. *Code of Canon Law*, Canon 900 § 2.

8. Cf. *Code of Canon Law*, Canon 249; Second Vatican Ecumenical Council, Constitution *Sacrosanctum Concilium*, 36; Declaration *Optatam totius*, 13.

pastoral needs suggest it, the opportunity to learn the *forma extraordinaria* of the Roman Rite.

22. In Dioceses without qualified priests, Diocesan Bishops can request assistance from priests of the Institutes erected by the Pontifical Commission *Ecclesia Dei*, either to the celebrate the *forma extraordinaria* or to teach others how to celebrate it.

23. The faculty to celebrate *sine populo* (or with the participation of only one minister) in the *forma extraordinaria* of the Roman Rite is given by the Motu Proprio to all priests, whether secular or religious (cf. Motu Proprio *Summorum Pontificum*, art. 2). For such celebrations therefore, priests, by provision of the Motu Proprio *Summorum Pontificum*, do not require any special permission from their Ordinaries or superiors.

Liturgical and Ecclesiastical Discipline

24. The liturgical books of the *forma extraordinaria* are to be used as they are. All those who wish to celebrate according to the *forma extraordinaria* of the Roman Rite must know the pertinent rubrics and are obliged to follow them correctly.

25. New saints and certain of the new prefaces can and ought to be inserted into the 1962 Missal[9], according to provisions which will be indicated subsequently.

---

9. BENEDICTUS XVI, *Epistola ad Episcopos ad producendas Litteras Apostolicas motu proprio datas, de Usu Liturgiae Romanae Instaurationi anni 1970 praecedentis*, AAS 99 (2007) 797.

26. As foreseen by article 6 of the Motu Proprio *Summorum Pontificum*, the readings of the Holy Mass of the Missal of 1962 can be proclaimed either solely in the Latin language, or in Latin followed by the vernacular or, in Low Masses, solely in the vernacular.

27. With regard to the disciplinary norms connected to celebration, the ecclesiastical discipline contained in the *Code of Canon Law* of 1983 applies.

28. Furthermore, by virtue of its character of special law, within its own area, the Motu Proprio *Summorum Pontificum* derogates from those provisions of law, connected with the sacred Rites, promulgated from 1962 onwards and incompatible with the rubrics of the liturgical books in effect in 1962.

Confirmation and Holy Orders

29. Permission to use the older formula for the rite of Confirmation was confirmed by the Motu Proprio *Summorum Pontificum* (cf. art. 9 § 2). Therefore, in the *forma extraordinaria*, it is not necessary to use the newer formula of Pope Paul VI as found in the *Ordo Confirmationis*.

30. As regards tonsure, minor orders and the subdiaconate, the Motu Proprio *Summorum Pontificum* does not introduce any change in the discipline of the *Code of Canon Law* of 1983; consequently, in Institutes of Consecrated Life and Societies of Apostolic Life which

are under the Pontifical Commission *Ecclesia Dei*, one who has made solemn profession or who has been definitively incorporated into a clerical institute of apostolic life, becomes incardinated as a cleric in the institute or society upon ordination to the diaconate, in accordance with canon 266 § 2 of the *Code of Canon Law*.

31. Only in Institutes of Consecrated Life and Societies of Apostolic Life which are under the Pontifical Commission Ecclesia Dei, and in those which use the liturgical books of the *forma extraordinaria*, is the use of the *Pontificale Romanum* of 1962 for the conferral of minor and major orders permitted.

Breviarium Romanum

32. Art. 9 § 3 of the Motu Proprio *Summorum Pontificum* gives clerics the faculty to use the *Breviarium Romanum* in effect in 1962, which is to be prayed entirely and in the Latin language.

The Sacred Triduum

33. If there is a qualified priest, a *coetus fidelium* ("group of faithful"), which follows the older liturgical tradition, can also celebrate the Sacred *Triduum* in the *forma extraordinaria*. When there is no church or oratory designated exclusively for such celebrations, the parish priest or Ordinary, in agreement with the qualified priest,

should find some arrangement favourable to the good of souls, not excluding the possibility of a repetition of the celebration of the Sacred Triduum in the same church.

The Rites of Religious Orders

34. The use of the liturgical books proper to the Religious Orders which were in effect in 1962 is permitted.

Pontificale Romanum and the *Rituale Romanum*

35. The use of the *Pontificale Romanum*, the *Rituale Romanum*, as well as the *Caeremoniale Episcoporum* in effect in 1962, is permitted, in keeping with n. 28 of this Instruction, and always respecting n. 31 of the same Instruction.

The Holy Father Pope Benedict XVI, in an audience granted to the undersigned Cardinal President of the Pontifical Commission Ecclesia Dei *on 8 April 2011, approved this present Instruction and ordered its publication.*

Given at Rome, at the Offices of the Pontifical Commission *Ecclesia Dei*, 30 April, 2011, on the memorial of Pope Saint Pius V.

William Cardinal Levada
President

Mons. Guido Pozzo
Secretary

LITTERAE APOSTOLICAE
MOTU PROPRIO DATAE
BENEDICTUS XVI

Summorum Pontificum cura ad hoc tempus usque semper fuit, ut Christi Ecclesia Divinae Maiestati cultum dignum offerret, "ad laudem et gloriam nominis Sui" et "ad utilitatem totius Ecclesiae Suae sanctae".

Ab immemorabili tempore sicut etiam in futurum, principium servandum est "iuxta quod unaquaeque Ecclesia particularis concordare debet cum universali Ecclesia non solum quoad fidei doctrinam et signa sacramentalia, sed etiam quoad usus universaliter acceptos ab apostolica et continua traditione, qui servandi sunt non solum ut errores vitentur, verum etiam ad fidei integritatem tradendam, quia Ecclesiae lex orandi eius legi credendi respondet"[1].

Inter Pontifices qui talem debitam curam adhibuerunt, nomen excellit sancti Gregorii Magni, qui tam fidem catholicam quam thesauros cultus ac culturae a Romanis in saeculis praecedentibus cumulatos novis Europae populis transmittendos curavit. Sacrae Liturgiae tam Missae Sacrificii quam Officii Divini formam, uti in Urbe celebrabatur, definiri conservarique iussit. Monachos

---

[1] *Institutio generalis Missalis Romani*, Editio tertia, 2002, 397.

quoque et moniales maxime fovit, qui sub Regula sancti Benedicti militantes, ubique simul cum Evangelii annuntiatione illam quoque saluberrimam Regulae sententiam vita sua illustrarunt, "ut operi Dei nihil praeponatur" (cap. 43). Tali modo sacra liturgia secundum morem Romanum non solum fidem et pietatem sed et culturam multarum gentium fecundavit. Constat utique liturgiam latinam variis suis formis Ecclesiae in omnibus aetatis christianae saeculis permultos Sanctos in vita spirituali stimulasse atque tot populos in religionis virtute roborasse ac eorundem pietatem fecundasse.

Ut autem Sacra Liturgia hoc munus efficacius expleret, plures alii Romani Pontifices decursu saeculorum peculiarem sollicitudinem impenderunt, inter quos eminet Sanctus Pius V, qui magno cum studio pastorali, Concilio Tridentino exhortante, totum Ecclesiae cultum innovavit, librorum liturgicorum emendatorum et "ad normam Patrum instauratorum" editionem curavit eosque Ecclesiae latinae usui dedit.

Inter Ritus romani libros liturgicos patet eminere Missale Romanum, quod in romana urbe succrevit, atque succedentibus saeculis gradatim formas assumpsit, quae cum illa in generationibus recentioribus vigente magnam habent similitudinem.

"Quod idem omnino propositum tempore progrediente Pontifices Romani sunt persecuti, cum novas ad aetates accommodaverunt aut ritus librosque liturgicos determinaverunt, ac deinde cum ineunte hoc nostro saeculo ampliorem iam complexi sunt redintegrationem"[2]. Sic vero egerunt Decessores nostri Clemens VIII, Urbanus VIII, sanctus Pius X[3], Benedictus XV, Pius XII et beatus Ioannes XXIII.

Recentioribus autem temporibus, Concilium Vaticanum II desiderium expressit, ut debita observantia et reverentia erga cultum divinum denuo instauraretur ac necessitatibus nostrae aetatis aptaretur. Quo desiderio motus, Decessor noster Summus Pontifex Paulus VI libros liturgicos instauratos et partim innovatos anno 1970 Ecclesiae latinae approbavit; qui ubique terrarum permultas in linguas vulgares conversi, ab Episcopis atque a sacerdotibus et fidelibus libenter recepti sunt. Ioannes Paulus II tertiam editionem typicam Missalis Romani recognovit. Sic Romani Pontifices operati sunt ut "hoc quasi aedificium liturgicum [...] rursus, dignitate splendidum et concinnitate" appareret[4].

Aliquibus autem in regionibus haud pauci fideles antecedentibus formis liturgicis, quae eorum culturam

---

[2] Ioannes Paulus Pp. II, Litt. ap. *Vicesimus quintus annus* (4 Decembris 1988), 3: AAS 81 (1989), 899.

[3] *Ibid.*

[4] Pius Pp. X, Litt. Ap. Motu proprio datae *Abhinc duos annos* (23 Octobris 1913): AAS 5 (1913), 449-450; cfr Ioannes Paulus II, Litt. ap. *Vicesimus quintus annus* (4 Decembris 1988), 3: AAS 81 (1989), 899.

et spiritum tam profunde imbuerant, tanto amore et affectu adhaeserunt et adhaerere pergunt, ut Summus Pontifex Ioannes Paulus II, horum fidelium pastorali cura motus, anno 1984 speciali Indulto "Quattuor abhinc annos", a Congregatione pro Cultu Divino exarato, facultatem concessit utendi Missali Romano a Ioanne XXIII anno 1962 edito; anno autem 1988 Ioannes Paulus II iterum, litteris Apostolicis "Ecclesia Dei" Motu proprio datis, Episcopos exhortatus est ut talem facultatem late et generose in favorem omnium fidelium id petentium adhiberent.

Instantibus precibus horum fidelium iam a Praedecessore Nostro Ioanne Paulo II diu perpensis, auditis etiam a Nobis Patribus Cardinalibus in Concistorio die XXIII mensis martii anni 2006 habito, omnibus mature perpensis, invocato Spiritu Sancto et Dei freti auxilio, praesentibus Litteris Apostolicis DECERNIMUS quae sequuntur:

Art. 1. Missale Romanum a Paulo VI promulgatum ordinaria expressio "Legis orandi" Ecclesiae catholicae ritus latini est. Missale autem Romanum a S. Pio V promulgatum et a B. Ioanne XXIII denuo editum habeatur uti extraordinaria expressio eiusdem "Legis orandi" Ecclesiae et ob venerabilem et antiquum eius usum debito gaudeat honore. Hae duae expressiones "legis orandi" Ecclesiae, minime vero inducent in divisionem "legis credendi" Ecclesiae; sunt enim duo usus unici ritus romani.

Proinde Missae Sacrificium, iuxta editionem typicam Missalis Romani a B. Ioanne XXIII anno 1962 promulgatam et numquam abrogatam, uti formam extraordinariam Liturgiae Ecclesiae, celebrare licet. Conditiones vero a documentis antecedentibus "Quattuor abhinc annos" et "Ecclesia Dei" pro usu huius Missalis statutae, substituuntur ut sequitur:

Art. 2. In Missis sine populo celebratis, quilibet sacerdos catholicus ritus latini, sive saecularis sive religiosus, uti potest aut Missali Romano a beato Papa Ioanne XXIII anno 1962 edito, aut Missali Romano a Summo Pontifice Paulo VI anno 1970 promulgato, et quidem qualibet die, excepto Triduo Sacro. Ad talem celebrationem secundum unum alterumve Missale, sacerdos nulla eget licentia, nec Sedis Apostolicae nec Ordinarii sui.

Art. 3. Si communitates Institutorum vitae consecratae atque Societatum vitae apostolicae iuris sive pontificii sive dioecesani quae in celebratione conventuali seu "communitatis" in oratoriis propriis celebrationem sanctae Missae iuxta editionem Missalis Romani anno 1962 promulgatam habere cupiunt, id eis licet. Si singula communitas aut totum Institutum vel Societas tales celebrationes saepe vel plerumque vel permanenter perficere vult, res a Superioribus maioribus ad normam iuris et secundum leges et statuta particularia decernatur.

Art. 4. Ad celebrationes sanctae Missae de quibus supra in art. 2 admitti possunt, servatis de iure servandis, etiam christifideles qui sua sponte id petunt.

Art. 5, § 1. In paroeciis, ubi coetus fidelium traditioni liturgicae antecedenti adhaerentium continenter exsistit, parochus eorum petitiones ad celebrandam sanctam Missam iuxta ritum Missalis Romani anno 1962 editi, libenter suscipiat. Ipse videat ut harmonice concordetur bonum horum fidelium cum ordinaria paroeciae pastorali cura, sub Episcopi regimine ad normam canonis 392, discordiam vitando et totius Ecclesiae unitatem fovendo.

§ 2. Celebratio secundum Missale B. Ioannis XXIII locum habere potest diebus ferialibus; dominicis autem et festis una etiam celebratio huiusmodi fieri potest.

§ 3. Fidelibus seu sacerdotibus id petentibus, parochus celcbrationes, hac in forma extraordinaria, permittat etiam in adiunctis peculiaribus, uti sunt matrimonia, exsequiae aut celebrationes occasionales, verbi gratia peregrinationes.

§ 4. Sacerdotes Missali B. Ioannis XXIII utentes, idonei esse debent ac iure non impediti.

§ 5. In ecclesiis, quae non sunt nec paroeciales nec conventuales, Rectoris ecclesiae est concedere licentiam de qua supra.

Art. 6. In Missis iuxta Missale B. Ioannis XXIII celebratis cum populo, Lectiones proclamari possunt etiam lingua vernacula, utendo editionibus ab Apostolica Sede recognitis.

Art. 7. Ubi aliquis coetus fidelium laicorum, de quo in art. 5 § 1 petita a parocho non obtinuerit, de re certiorem faciat Episcopum dioecesanum. Episcopus enixe rogatur ut eorum optatum exaudiat. Si ille ad huiusmodi celebrationem providere non potest res ad Pontificiam Commissionem "Ecclesia Dei" referatur.

Art. 8. Episcopus, qui vult providere huiusmodi petitionibus christifidelium laicorum, sed ob varias causas impeditur, rem Pontificiae Commissioni "Ecclesia Dei" committere potest, quae ei consilium et auxilium dabit.

Art. 9, § 1. Parochus item, omnibus bene perpensis, licentiam concedere potest utendi rituali antiquiore in administrandis sacramentis Baptismatis, Matrimonii, Poenitentiae et Unctionis Infirmorum, bono animarum id suadente.

§ 2. Ordinariis autem facultas conceditur celebrandi Confirmationis sacramentum utendo Pontificali Romano antiquo, bono animarum id suadente.

§ 3. Fas est clericis in sacris constitutis uti etiam Breviario Romano a B. Ioanne XXIII anno 1962 promulgato.

Art 10. Fas est Ordinario loci, si opportunum iudicaverit, paroeciam personalem ad normam canonis 518 pro celebrationibus iuxta formam antiquiorem ritus romani erigere aut rectorem vel cappellanum nominare, servatis de iure servandis.

Art. 11. Pontificia Commissio "Ecclesia Dei" a Ioanne Paulo II anno 1988 erecta[5], munus suum adimplere pergit.

Quae Commissio formam, officia et normas agendi habeat, quae Romanus Pontifex ipsi attribuere voluerit.

Art. 12. Eadem Commissio, ultra facultates quibus iam gaudet, auctoritatem Sanctae Sedis exercebit, vigilando de observantia et applicatione harum dispositionum.

Quaecumque vero a Nobis hisce Litteris Apostolicis Motu proprio datis decreta sunt, ea omnia firma ac rata esse et a die decima quarta Septembris huius anni, in festo Exaltationis Sanctae Crucis, servari iubemus, contrariis quibuslibet rebus non obstantibus.

Datum Romae, apud Sanctum Petrum, die septima mensis Iulii, anno Domini MMVII, Pontificatus Nostri tertio.

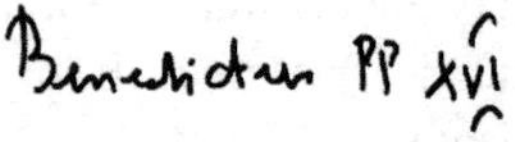

BENEDICTUS PP. XVI

---

[5] Cfr Ioannes Paulus Pp. II, Litt. ap. Motu proprio datae *Ecclesia Dei* (2 iulii 1988), 6: AAS 80 (1988), 1498.

MOTU PROPRIO "SUMMORUM PONTIFICUM"

Up to our own times, it has been the constant concern of supreme pontiffs to ensure that the Church of Christ offers a worthy ritual to the Divine Majesty, 'to the praise and glory of His name,' and 'to the benefit of all His Holy Church.'

Since time immemorial it has been necessary - as it is also for the future - to maintain the principle according to which 'each particular Church must concur with the universal Church, not only as regards the doctrine of the faith and the sacramental signs, but also as regards the usages universally accepted by uninterrupted apostolic tradition, which must be observed not only to avoid errors but also to transmit the integrity of the faith, because the Church's law of prayer corresponds to her law of faith.'[1]

Among the pontiffs who showed that requisite concern, particularly outstanding is the name of St Gregory the Great, who made every effort to ensure that the new peoples of Europe received both the Catholic faith and the treasures of worship and culture that had been accumulated by the Romans in preceding centuries. He commanded that the form of the sacred liturgy as celebrated in Rome (concerning both the Sacrifice of the

---

[1] *General Instruction of the Roman Missal*, 3rd ed., 2002, no. 397.

Mass and the Divine Office) be conserved. He took great concern to ensure the dissemination of monks and nuns who, following the Rule of St Benedict, together with the announcement of the Gospel illustrated with their lives the wise provision of their Rule that 'nothing should be placed before the work of God.' In this way the sacred liturgy, celebrated according to the Roman use, enriched not only the faith and piety but also the culture of many peoples. It is known, in fact, that the Latin liturgy of the Church in its various forms, in each century of the Christian era, has been a spur to the spiritual life of many saints, has reinforced many peoples in the virtue of religion and fecundated their piety.

Many other Roman pontiffs, in the course of the centuries, showed particular solicitude in ensuring that the sacred liturgy accomplished this task more effectively. Outstanding among them is St Pius V who, sustained by great pastoral zeal and following the exhortations of the Council of Trent, renewed the entire liturgy of the Church, oversaw the publication of liturgical books amended and 'renewed in accordance with the norms of the Fathers,' and provided them for the use of the Latin Church.

One of the liturgical books of the Roman rite is the Roman Missal, which developed in the city of Rome and, with the passing of the centuries, little by little took forms very similar to that it has had in recent times.

'It was towards this same goal that succeeding Roman Pontiffs directed their energies during the subsequent centuries in order to ensure that the rites and liturgical books were brought up to date and when necessary clarified. From the beginning of this century they undertook a more general reform.'[2] Thus our predecessors Clement VIII, Urban VIII, St Pius X[3], Benedict XV, Pius XII and Blessed John XXIII all played a part.

In more recent times, Vatican Council II expressed a desire that the respectful reverence due to divine worship should be renewed and adapted to the needs of our time. Moved by this desire our predecessor, the Supreme Pontiff Paul VI, approved, in 1970, reformed and partly renewed liturgical books for the Latin Church. These, translated into the various languages of the world, were willingly accepted by bishops, priests and faithful. John Paul II amended the third typical edition of the Roman Missal. Thus Roman pontiffs have operated to ensure that 'this kind of liturgical edifice...should again appear resplendent for its dignity and harmony.'[4]

---

[2] John Paul II, Apostolic Letter "*Vicesimus quintus annus*," 4th December 1988, 3: AAS 81 (1989), 899.

[3] *Ibid.*

[4] St Pius X, Apostolic Letter Motu propio data, "*Abhinc duos annos*," 23rd October 1913: AAS 5 (1913), 449-450; cf John Paul II, Apostolic Letter "*Vicesimus quintus annus*," no. 3: AAS 81 (1989), 899.

But in some regions, no small numbers of faithful adhered and continue to adhere with great love and affection to the earlier liturgical forms. These had so deeply marked their culture and their spirit that in 1984 the Supreme Pontiff John Paul II, moved by a concern for the pastoral care of these faithful, with the special indult 'Quattuor abhinc anno," issued by the Congregation for Divine Worship, granted permission to use the Roman Missal published by Blessed John XXIII in the year 1962. Later, in the year 1988, John Paul II with the Apostolic Letter given as Motu Proprio, 'Ecclesia Dei,' exhorted bishops to make generous use of this power in favor of all the faithful who so desired.

Following the insistent prayers of these faithful, long deliberated upon by our predecessor John Paul II, and after having listened to the views of the Cardinal Fathers of the Consistory of 22nd March 2006, having reflected deeply upon all aspects of the question, invoked the Holy Spirit and trusting in the help of God, with these Apostolic Letters we establish the following:

Art 1. The Roman Missal promulgated by Paul VI is the ordinary expression of the 'Lex orandi' (Law of prayer) of the Catholic Church of the Latin rite. Nonetheless, the Roman Missal promulgated by St Pius V and reissued by Bl. John XXIII is to be considered as an extraordinary expression of that same 'Lex orandi,' and must be given due honour for its venerable and ancient usage. These two expressions of the Church's Lex orandi will in no way lead to a division in the Church's 'Lex credendi' (Law of belief). They are, in fact two usages of the one Roman rite.

It is, therefore, permissible to celebrate the Sacrifice of the Mass following the typical edition of the Roman Missal promulgated by Bl. John XXIII in 1962 and never abrogated, as an extraordinary form of the Liturgy of the Church. The conditions for the use of this Missal as laid down by earlier documents 'Quattuor abhinc annis' and 'Ecclesia Dei,' are substituted as follows:

Art. 2. In Masses celebrated without the people, each Catholic priest of the Latin rite, whether secular or regular, may use the Roman Missal published by Bl. Pope John XXIII in 1962, or the Roman Missal promulgated by Pope Paul VI in 1970, and may do so on any day with the exception of the Easter Triduum. For such celebrations, with either one Missal or the other, the priest has no need for permission from the Apostolic See or from his Ordinary.

Art. 3. Communities of Institutes of consecrated life and of Societies of apostolic life, of either pontifical or diocesan right, wishing to celebrate Mass in accordance with the edition of the Roman Missal promulgated in 1962, for conventual or "community" celebration in their oratories, may do so. If an individual community or an entire Institute or Society wishes to undertake such celebrations often, habitually or permanently, the decision must be taken by the Superiors Major, in accordance with the law and following their own specific decrees and statues.

Art. 4. Celebrations of Mass as mentioned above in art. 2 may - observing all the norms of law - also be attended by faithful who, of their own free will, ask to be admitted.

Art. 5. § 1. In parishes, where there is a stable group of faithful who adhere to the earlier liturgical tradition, the pastor should willingly accept their requests to celebrate the Mass according to the rite of the Roman Missal published in 1962, and ensure that the welfare of these faithful harmonises with the ordinary pastoral care of the parish, under the guidance of the bishop in accordance with canon 392, avoiding discord and favouring the unity of the whole Church.

§ 2. Celebration in accordance with the Missal of Bl. John XXIII may take place on working days; while on Sundays and feast days one such celebration may also be held.

§ 3. For faithful and priests who request it, the pastor should also allow celebrations in this extraordinary form for special circumstances such as marriages, funerals or occasional celebrations, e.g. pilgrimages.

§ 4. Priests who use the Missal of Bl. John XXIII must be qualified to do so and not juridically impeded.

§ 5. In churches that are not parish or conventual churches, it is the duty of the Rector of the church to grant the above permission.

Art. 6. In Masses celebrated in the presence of the people in accordance with the Missal of Bl. John XXIII, the readings may be given in the vernacular, using editions recognised by the Apostolic See.

Art. 7. If a group of lay faithful, as mentioned in art. 5 § 1, has not obtained satisfaction to their requests from the pastor, they should inform the diocesan bishop. The bishop is strongly requested to satisfy their wishes. If he cannot arrange for such celebration to take place, the matter should be referred to the Pontifical Commission "Ecclesia Dei".

Art. 8. A bishop who, desirous of satisfying such requests, but who for various reasons is unable to do so, may refer the problem to the Commission "Ecclesia Dei" to obtain counsel and assistance.

Art. 9. § 1. The pastor, having attentively examined all aspects, may also grant permission to use the earlier ritual for the administration of the Sacraments of Baptism, Marriage, Penance, and the Anointing of the Sick, if the good of souls would seem to require it.

§ 2. Ordinaries are given the right to celebrate the Sacrament of Confirmation using the earlier Roman Pontifical, if the good of souls would seem to require it.

§ 3. Clerics ordained "in sacris constitutis" may use the Roman Breviary promulgated by Bl. John XXIII in 1962.

Art. 10. The ordinary of a particular place, if he feels it appropriate, may erect a personal parish in accordance with can. 518 for celebrations following the ancient form of the Roman rite, or appoint a chaplain, while observing all the norms of law.

Art. 11. The Pontifical Commission "Ecclesia Dei", erected by John Paul II in 1988[5], continues to exercise its function. Said Commission will have the form, duties and norms that the Roman Pontiff wishes to assign it.

Art. 12. This Commission, apart from the powers it enjoys, will exercise the authority of the Holy See, supervising the observance and application of these dispositions.

---

[5] Cf John Paul II, Apostolic Letter Motu proprio data "*Ecclesia Dei*," 2nd July 1988, 6: AAS 80 (1988), 1498.

We order that everything We have established with these Apostolic Letters issued as Motu Proprio be considered as "established and decreed", and to be observed from 14th September of this year, Feast of the Exaltation of the Cross, whatever there may be to the contrary.

From Rome, at St Peter's, 7th July 2007, third year of Our Pontificate.

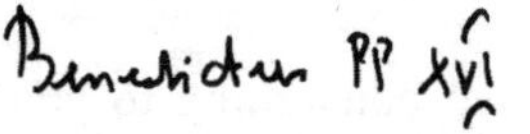

BENEDICTUS PP. XVI

The English text is reproduced from an unofficial translation provided by the Vatican Information Service.

Letter of His Holiness Benedict XVI to the Bishops on the occasion of the publication of the Apostolic Letter "Motu Proprio Data" *Summorum Pontificum* on the use of the Roman Liturgy prior to the reform of 1970

My dear Brother Bishops,

With great trust and hope, I am consigning to you as Pastors the text of a new Apostolic Letter "*Motu Proprio data*" on the use of the Roman liturgy prior to the reform of 1970. The document is the fruit of much reflection, numerous consultations and prayer.

News reports and judgments made without sufficient information have created no little confusion. There have been very divergent reactions ranging from joyful acceptance to harsh opposition, about a plan whose contents were in reality unknown.

This document was most directly opposed on account of two fears, which I would like to address somewhat more closely in this letter.

In the first place, there is the fear that the document detracts from the authority of the Second Vatican Council, one of whose essential decisions – the liturgical reform – is being called into question.

This fear is unfounded. In this regard, it must first be said that the Missal published by Paul VI and then republished in two subsequent editions by John Paul II, obviously is and continues to be the normal Form – the *Forma ordinaria* – of the Eucharistic Liturgy. The last version of the *Missale Romanum* prior to the Council, which was published with the authority of Pope John XXIII in 1962 and used during the Council, will now be able to be used as a *Forma extraordinaria* of the liturgical celebration. It is not appropriate to speak of these two versions of the Roman Missal as if they were "two Rites". Rather, it is a matter of a twofold use of one and the same rite.

As for the use of the 1962 Missal as a *Forma extraordinaria* of the liturgy of the Mass, I would like to draw attention to the fact that this Missal was never juridically abrogated and, consequently, in principle, was always permitted. At the time of the introduction of the new Missal, it did not seem necessary to issue specific norms for the possible use of the earlier Missal. Probably it was thought that it would be a matter of a few individual cases which would be resolved, case by case, on the local level. Afterwards, however, it soon became apparent that a good number of people remained strongly attached to this usage of the Roman Rite, which had been familiar to them from childhood. This was especially the case in countries where the liturgical movement had provided many people with a notable liturgical formation and a deep, personal familiarity with the earlier Form of the liturgical celebration. We all know that, in the movement led by Archbishop Lefebvre, fidelity to the old Missal became an external mark of identity; the reasons for the break which arose over this, however, were at a deeper level. Many people who clearly accepted the binding character of the Second Vatican Council, and were faithful to the Pope and the Bishops, nonetheless also desired to recover the form of the sacred liturgy that was dear to them. This occurred above all because in many places celebrations were not faithful to the prescriptions of the new Missal, but the latter actually was understood as authorizing or even requiring creativity, which frequently led to deformations of the liturgy which were hard to bear. I am speaking from experience, since I too lived through that period with all its hopes and its confusion. And I have seen how arbitrary deformations of the liturgy caused deep pain to individuals totally rooted in the faith of the Church.

Pope John Paul II thus felt obliged to provide, in his *Motu Proprio Ecclesia Dei* (2nd July 1988), guidelines for the use of the 1962 Missal; that document, however, did not contain detailed prescriptions but appealed in a general way to the generous response of Bishops towards the "legitimate aspirations" of those members of the faithful who requested this usage of the Roman Rite. At the time, the Pope primarily wanted to assist the Society of Saint Pius X to recover full unity with the Successor of Peter, and sought to heal a wound experienced ever more painfully. Unfortunately this reconciliation has not yet come about. Nonetheless, a number of communities have gratefully made use of the possibilities provided by the *Motu Proprio*. On the other hand, difficulties remain concerning the use of the 1962 Missal outside of these groups, because of the lack of precise juridical norms, particularly because Bishops, in such cases, frequently feared that the authority of the Council would be called into question. Immediately after the Second Vatican Council it was presumed that requests for the use of the 1962 Missal would be limited to the older generation which had grown up with it, but in the meantime it has clearly been demonstrated that young persons too have discovered this liturgical form, felt its attraction and found in it a form of encounter with the Mystery of the Most Holy Eucharist, particularly suited to them. Thus the need has arisen for a clearer juridical regulation which had not been foreseen at the time of the 1988 Motu Proprio. The present Norms are also meant to free Bishops from constantly having to evaluate anew how they are to respond to various situations.

In the second place, the fear was expressed in discussions about the awaited *Motu Proprio*, that the possibility of a wider use of the 1962 Missal would lead to disarray or even divisions within parish communities. This fear also strikes me as quite unfounded. The use of the old Missal presupposes a certain degree of liturgical formation and some knowledge of the Latin language; neither of these is found very often. Already from these concrete presuppositions, it is clearly seen that the new Missal will certainly remain the ordinary Form of the Roman Rite, not only on account of the juridical norms, but also because of the actual situation of the communities of the faithful.

It is true that there have been exaggerations and at times social aspects unduly linked to the attitude of the faithful attached to the ancient Latin liturgical tradition. Your charity and pastoral prudence will be an incentive and guide for improving these. For that matter, the two Forms of the usage of the Roman Rite can be mutually enriching: new Saints and some of the new Prefaces can and should be inserted in the old Missal. The "*Ecclesia Dei*" Commission, in contact with various bodies devoted to the *usus antiquior*, will study the practical possibilities in this regard. The celebration of the Mass according to the Missal of Paul VI will be able to demonstrate, more powerfully than has been the case hitherto, the sacrality which attracts many people to the former usage. The most sure guarantee that the Missal of Paul VI can unite parish communities and be loved by them consists in its being celebrated with great reverence in harmony with the liturgical directives.

This will bring out the spiritual richness and the theological depth of this Missal.

I now come to the positive reason which motivated my decision to issue this *Motu Proprio* updating that of 1988. It is a matter of coming to an interior reconciliation in the heart of the Church. Looking back over the past, to the divisions which in the course of the centuries have rent the Body of Christ, one continually has the impression that, at critical moments when divisions were coming about, not enough was done by the Church's leaders to maintain or regain reconciliation and unity. One has the impression that omissions on the part of the Church have had their share of blame for the fact that these divisions were able to harden. This glance at the past imposes an obligation on us today: to make every effort to unable for all those who truly desire unity to remain in that unity or to attain it anew. I think of a sentence in the Second Letter to the Corinthians, where Paul writes: "Our mouth is open to you, Corinthians; our heart is wide. You are not restricted by us, but you are restricted in your own affections. In return…widen your hearts also!" (2 *Cor* 6:11-13). Paul was certainly speaking in another context, but his exhortation can and must touch us too, precisely on this subject. Let us generously open our hearts and make room for everything that the faith itself allows.

There is no contradiction between the two editions of the Roman Missal. In the history of the liturgy there is growth and progress, but no rupture. What earlier generations held as sacred, remains sacred and great for us too, and it cannot be all of a sudden entirely forbidden or even considered harmful. It behooves all of us to preserve the riches which have developed in the Church's faith and prayer, and to give them their proper place. Needless to say, in order to experience full communion, the priests of the communities adhering to the former usage cannot, as a matter of principle, exclude celebrating according to the new books. The total exclusion of the new rite would not in fact be consistent with the recognition of its value and holiness.

In conclusion, dear Brothers, I very much wish to stress that these new norms do not in any way lessen your own authority and responsibility, either for the liturgy or for the pastoral care of your faithful. Each Bishop, in fact, is the moderator of the liturgy in his own Diocese (cf. *Sacrosanctum Concilium*, 22: "*Sacrae Liturgiae moderatio ab Ecclesiae auctoritate unice pendet quae quidem est apud Apostolicam Sedem et, ad normam iuris, apud Episcopum*").

Nothing is taken away, then, from the authority of the Bishop, whose role remains that of being watchful that all is done in peace and serenity. Should some problem arise which the parish priest cannot resolve, the local Ordinary will always be able to intervene, in full harmony, however, with all that has been laid down by the new norms of the *Motu Proprio*.

Furthermore, I invite you, dear Brothers, to send to the Holy See an account of your experiences, three years after this Motu Proprio has taken effect. If truly serious difficulties come to light, ways to remedy them can be sought.

Dear Brothers, with gratitude and trust, I entrust to your hearts as Pastors these pages and the norms of the *Motu Proprio*. Let us always be mindful of the words of the Apostle Paul addressed to the presbyters of Ephesus: "Take heed to yourselves and to all the flock, in which the Holy Spirit has made you overseers, to care for the Church of God which he obtained with the blood of his own Son" (*Ac* 20:28).

I entrust these norms to the powerful intercession of Mary, Mother of the Church, and I cordially impart my Apostolic Blessing to you, dear Brothers, to the parish priests of your dioceses, and to all the priests, your co-workers, as well as to all your faithful.

Given at Saint Peter's, 7th July 2007

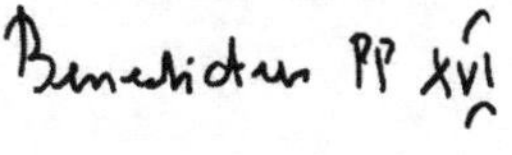

BENEDICTUS PP. XVI